50 Flavorful Fish and Seafood Dishes

By: Kelly Johnson

Table of Contents

- Grilled Lemon Herb Salmon
- Garlic Butter Shrimp
- Spicy Tuna Poke Bowl
- Baked Cod with Tomatoes and Olives
- Shrimp Tacos with Mango Salsa
- Honey Garlic Glazed Salmon
- Fish and Chips with Tartar Sauce
- Seafood Paella
- Cilantro Lime Grilled Fish
- Blackened Catfish
- Creamy Tuscan Garlic Salmon
- Lemon Dill Baked Tilapia
- Thai Coconut Curry Shrimp
- Herb-Crusted Halibut
- Teriyaki Salmon Skewers
- Clam Chowder
- Crab Cakes with Remoulade
- Pesto Baked Mahi-Mahi
- Fish Tacos with Chipotle Sauce
- Grilled Sardines with Lemon and Parsley
- Smoked Salmon Pasta
- Shrimp Scampi
- Stuffed Flounder with Spinach and Feta
- Lemon Garlic Butter Scallops
- Szechuan Spicy Shrimp
- Baked Barramundi with Herb Butter
- Coconut Shrimp with Sweet Chili Sauce
- Mediterranean Grilled Octopus
- Sesame Crusted Ahi Tuna
- Fish Curry with Coconut Milk
- Lobster Roll
- Crab Linguine with Garlic and Parsley
- Fish Tikka Masala
- Grilled Prawns with Garlic and Herbs
- Garlic Lemon Butter Mussels

- Baked Salmon with Dill Cream Sauce
- Fish en Papillote (Fish in Parchment)
- Shrimp Fried Rice
- Fish Stew with Fresh Herbs
- Lemon Herb Grilled Swordfish
- Crispy Fish Sandwiches
- Oysters Rockefeller
- Cajun Shrimp and Grits
- Grilled Fish Kebabs
- Thai Grilled Squid
- Pan-Seared Sea Bass
- Clams Casino
- Lobster Bisque
- Sautéed Garlic Shrimp with Spinach
- Miso Glazed Cod

Grilled Lemon Herb Salmon

Ingredients:

- 4 salmon fillets (6 ounces each)
- 2 tablespoons olive oil
- 2 tablespoons fresh lemon juice
- 2 teaspoons lemon zest
- 2 garlic cloves, minced
- 1 tablespoon fresh parsley, chopped
- 1 tablespoon fresh dill, chopped
- 1 teaspoon salt
- ½ teaspoon black pepper
- Lemon wedges (for serving)

Instructions:

1. **Marinate the Salmon:**
   - In a small bowl, whisk together the olive oil, lemon juice, lemon zest, minced garlic, parsley, dill, salt, and pepper.
   - Place the salmon fillets in a shallow dish and pour the marinade over them. Cover and refrigerate for at least 30 minutes (or up to 2 hours) to let the flavors meld.
2. **Preheat the Grill:**
   - Preheat your grill to medium-high heat. Make sure the grill grates are clean and lightly oiled to prevent sticking.
3. **Grill the Salmon:**
   - Remove the salmon from the marinade, allowing the excess to drip off. Discard the remaining marinade.
   - Place the salmon fillets skin-side down on the grill. Grill for about 5-6 minutes on one side, then carefully flip them over using a spatula. Grill for another 4-5 minutes, or until the salmon is cooked through and flakes easily with a fork.
4. **Serve:**
   - Remove the salmon from the grill and let it rest for a couple of minutes. Serve with lemon wedges on the side for an extra burst of citrus flavor.

Enjoy your Grilled Lemon Herb Salmon with your favorite sides!

Garlic Butter Shrimp

Ingredients:

- 1 pound large shrimp, peeled and deveined
- 4 tablespoons unsalted butter
- 4 cloves garlic, minced
- 1 teaspoon red pepper flakes (adjust to taste)
- Salt and pepper to taste
- 2 tablespoons fresh lemon juice
- 2 tablespoons chopped fresh parsley
- Lemon wedges for serving

Instructions:

1. **Sauté Garlic:** In a large skillet, melt the butter over medium heat. Add the minced garlic and red pepper flakes, sautéing until fragrant (about 1-2 minutes). Be careful not to burn the garlic.
2. **Cook Shrimp:** Add the shrimp to the skillet in a single layer. Season with salt and pepper. Cook for about 2-3 minutes on one side, then flip the shrimp and cook for another 2-3 minutes or until they turn pink and opaque.
3. **Add Lemon Juice:** Remove the skillet from heat and stir in the fresh lemon juice and chopped parsley.
4. **Serve:** Transfer the shrimp to a serving dish and drizzle with the remaining garlic butter from the pan. Serve with lemon wedges on the side.

Spicy Tuna Poke Bowl

Ingredients:

- 1 cup sushi rice
- 1 1/4 cups water
- 1 pound sushi-grade tuna, diced
- 2 tablespoons soy sauce
- 1 tablespoon sesame oil
- 1 teaspoon Sriracha (adjust to taste)
- 1 avocado, sliced
- 1/2 cucumber, thinly sliced
- 1 small carrot, julienned
- 2 green onions, sliced
- 1 tablespoon sesame seeds
- Seaweed salad (optional, for serving)
- Pickled ginger (optional, for serving)

Instructions:

1. **Cook Sushi Rice:** Rinse the sushi rice under cold water until the water runs clear. In a medium saucepan, combine the rice and water, bringing to a boil. Reduce heat to low, cover, and simmer for 20 minutes. Remove from heat and let it sit for another 10 minutes. Fluff with a fork.
2. **Prepare Tuna Mixture:** In a bowl, combine the diced tuna, soy sauce, sesame oil, and Sriracha. Gently toss to coat the tuna evenly.
3. **Assemble Poke Bowl:** In serving bowls, place a scoop of sushi rice at the bottom. Top with the spicy tuna mixture, avocado slices, cucumber, carrot, and green onions.
4. **Garnish and Serve:** Sprinkle sesame seeds on top and add seaweed salad and pickled ginger if desired. Enjoy your poke bowl immediately!

Baked Cod with Tomatoes and Olives

Ingredients:

- 4 cod fillets
- 2 cups cherry tomatoes, halved
- 1/2 cup Kalamata olives, pitted and sliced
- 3 cloves garlic, minced
- 2 tablespoons olive oil
- 1 teaspoon dried oregano
- Salt and pepper to taste
- Fresh parsley for garnish

Instructions:

1. **Preheat Oven:** Preheat the oven to 400°F (200°C).
2. **Prepare Baking Dish:** In a baking dish, combine cherry tomatoes, olives, garlic, olive oil, oregano, salt, and pepper. Mix well.
3. **Add Cod:** Place the cod fillets on top of the tomato mixture. Drizzle with additional olive oil and season with salt and pepper.
4. **Bake:** Bake in the preheated oven for 15-20 minutes, or until the fish flakes easily with a fork.
5. **Serve:** Garnish with fresh parsley and serve immediately.

Shrimp Tacos with Mango Salsa

Ingredients:

- 1 pound shrimp, peeled and deveined
- 1 tablespoon olive oil
- 1 teaspoon chili powder
- 1/2 teaspoon cumin
- Salt and pepper to taste
- 8 small corn tortillas
- 1 cup diced mango
- 1/2 red onion, diced
- 1 jalapeño, minced
- 1/4 cup chopped cilantro
- Juice of 1 lime

Instructions:

1. **Cook Shrimp:** In a skillet, heat olive oil over medium heat. Add shrimp, chili powder, cumin, salt, and pepper. Cook until shrimp are pink and cooked through, about 4-5 minutes.
2. **Prepare Mango Salsa:** In a bowl, combine mango, red onion, jalapeño, cilantro, lime juice, and salt. Mix well.
3. **Assemble Tacos:** Warm tortillas in a dry skillet. Fill each tortilla with shrimp and top with mango salsa.
4. **Serve:** Serve the tacos with lime wedges on the side.

Honey Garlic Glazed Salmon

Ingredients:

- 4 salmon fillets
- 1/4 cup honey
- 3 tablespoons soy sauce
- 3 cloves garlic, minced
- 1 tablespoon olive oil
- Salt and pepper to taste
- Sliced green onions for garnish

Instructions:

1. **Preheat Oven:** Preheat the oven to 375°F (190°C).
2. **Make Glaze:** In a small bowl, whisk together honey, soy sauce, garlic, olive oil, salt, and pepper.
3. **Glaze Salmon:** Place salmon fillets in a baking dish and pour the honey garlic glaze over the top.
4. **Bake:** Bake for 15-20 minutes or until the salmon is cooked through and flakes easily.
5. **Serve:** Garnish with sliced green onions and serve with your choice of sides.

Fish and Chips with Tartar Sauce

Ingredients:

- 1 pound white fish fillets (such as cod or haddock)
- 1 cup all-purpose flour
- 1 teaspoon baking powder
- 1 cup cold sparkling water
- Salt and pepper to taste
- Oil for frying
- 4 cups frozen French fries

Tartar Sauce:

- 1/2 cup mayonnaise
- 2 tablespoons pickle relish
- 1 tablespoon lemon juice
- Salt and pepper to taste

Instructions:

1. **Prepare Tartar Sauce:** In a small bowl, mix together mayonnaise, pickle relish, lemon juice, salt, and pepper. Set aside.
2. **Make Batter:** In a bowl, whisk together flour, baking powder, salt, and pepper. Slowly add sparkling water until smooth.
3. **Heat Oil:** In a deep fryer or large pot, heat oil to 350°F (175°C).
4. **Fry Fish:** Dip fish fillets into the batter, then carefully lower them into the hot oil. Fry for 4-5 minutes or until golden brown. Remove and drain on paper towels.
5. **Cook Fries:** Fry frozen French fries according to package instructions.
6. **Serve:** Serve fish and chips with tartar sauce on the side.

Seafood Paella

Ingredients:

- 2 tablespoons olive oil
- 1 onion, diced
- 3 cloves garlic, minced
- 1 bell pepper, diced
- 1 cup Arborio rice
- 1/2 teaspoon smoked paprika
- 1/4 teaspoon saffron threads
- 4 cups chicken or seafood broth
- 1 cup shrimp, peeled and deveined
- 1 cup mussels, cleaned
- 1 cup peas
- Salt and pepper to taste
- Lemon wedges for serving

Instructions:

1. **Sauté Vegetables:** In a large paella pan or skillet, heat olive oil over medium heat. Add onion, garlic, and bell pepper. Sauté until soft.
2. **Add Rice and Spices:** Stir in Arborio rice, smoked paprika, saffron, salt, and pepper. Cook for 2 minutes.
3. **Add Broth:** Pour in the broth and bring to a simmer. Cook for 10 minutes without stirring.
4. **Add Seafood:** Add shrimp and mussels to the pan. Cover and cook for an additional 5-7 minutes, until the seafood is cooked and mussels have opened.
5. **Finish and Serve:** Stir in peas and let sit for a few minutes. Serve with lemon wedges.

Cilantro Lime Grilled Fish

Ingredients:

- 4 fish fillets (such as tilapia or mahi-mahi)
- 1/4 cup olive oil
- Juice of 2 limes
- 1/4 cup chopped cilantro
- 2 cloves garlic, minced
- Salt and pepper to taste

Instructions:

1. **Marinate Fish:** In a bowl, whisk together olive oil, lime juice, cilantro, garlic, salt, and pepper. Add fish fillets and marinate for at least 30 minutes.
2. **Preheat Grill:** Preheat the grill to medium-high heat.
3. **Grill Fish:** Remove fish from marinade and grill for 4-5 minutes on each side, or until cooked through and flaky.
4. **Serve:** Serve with additional lime wedges and a sprinkle of fresh cilantro.

Blackened Catfish

Ingredients:

- 4 catfish fillets
- 2 tablespoons paprika
- 1 teaspoon cayenne pepper
- 1 teaspoon garlic powder
- 1 teaspoon onion powder
- 1 teaspoon dried thyme
- 1 teaspoon salt
- 1/2 teaspoon black pepper
- 2 tablespoons butter
- Lemon wedges for serving

Instructions:

1. **Make Spice Mixture:** In a bowl, mix paprika, cayenne, garlic powder, onion powder, thyme, salt, and black pepper.
2. **Coat Fish:** Pat catfish fillets dry and coat both sides with the spice mixture.
3. **Heat Skillet:** In a skillet, melt butter over medium-high heat.
4. **Cook Fish:** Add the catfish fillets and cook for 3-4 minutes on each side until blackened and cooked through.
5. **Serve:** Serve with lemon wedges on the side.

Creamy Tuscan Garlic Salmon

Ingredients:

- 4 salmon fillets
- Salt and pepper to taste
- 2 tablespoons olive oil
- 4 cloves garlic, minced
- 1 cup heavy cream
- 1 cup cherry tomatoes, halved
- 1/2 cup spinach
- 1/4 cup grated Parmesan cheese
- Fresh basil for garnish

Instructions:

1. **Season Salmon:** Season salmon fillets with salt and pepper.
2. **Sear Salmon:** In a skillet, heat olive oil over medium heat. Add salmon fillets and cook for 4-5 minutes on each side until cooked through. Remove and set aside.
3. **Make Creamy Sauce:** In the same skillet, add garlic and sauté until fragrant. Add heavy cream, cherry tomatoes, spinach, and Parmesan cheese. Simmer until the sauce thickens.
4. **Combine:** Return salmon to the skillet and coat with the sauce.
5. **Serve:** Garnish with fresh basil and serve immediately.

Enjoy cooking these delightful seafood dishes!

Lemon Dill Baked Tilapia

Ingredients:

- 4 tilapia fillets
- 2 tablespoons olive oil
- Juice of 1 lemon
- 2 teaspoons fresh dill, chopped (or 1 teaspoon dried)
- Salt and pepper to taste
- Lemon slices for garnish

Instructions:

1. **Preheat Oven:** Preheat the oven to 400°F (200°C).
2. **Prepare Baking Dish:** Place the tilapia fillets in a greased baking dish. Drizzle with olive oil and lemon juice.
3. **Season:** Sprinkle with dill, salt, and pepper. Place lemon slices on top of the fillets.
4. **Bake:** Bake for 15-20 minutes, or until the fish flakes easily with a fork.
5. **Serve:** Garnish with additional fresh dill and lemon slices.

Thai Coconut Curry Shrimp

Ingredients:

- 1 pound shrimp, peeled and deveined
- 1 tablespoon olive oil
- 1 onion, diced
- 2 cloves garlic, minced
- 1 tablespoon ginger, minced
- 1 tablespoon red curry paste
- 1 can (14 oz) coconut milk
- 1 cup bell peppers, sliced
- 1 cup snap peas
- Salt to taste
- Fresh cilantro for garnish

Instructions:

1. **Sauté Aromatics:** In a large skillet, heat olive oil over medium heat. Add onion, garlic, and ginger, sautéing until fragrant.
2. **Add Curry Paste:** Stir in red curry paste and cook for an additional minute.
3. **Add Coconut Milk:** Pour in coconut milk and bring to a simmer.
4. **Cook Shrimp and Vegetables:** Add shrimp, bell peppers, and snap peas. Cook until shrimp are pink and vegetables are tender, about 5-7 minutes.
5. **Serve:** Season with salt and garnish with fresh cilantro. Serve over rice or noodles.

Herb-Crusted Halibut

Ingredients:

- 4 halibut fillets
- 1/2 cup breadcrumbs
- 1/4 cup fresh parsley, chopped
- 1 tablespoon fresh thyme, chopped
- 1 tablespoon olive oil
- Salt and pepper to taste
- Lemon wedges for serving

Instructions:

1. **Preheat Oven:** Preheat the oven to 425°F (220°C).
2. **Prepare Crust Mixture:** In a bowl, combine breadcrumbs, parsley, thyme, olive oil, salt, and pepper.
3. **Coat Halibut:** Place halibut fillets on a baking sheet and press the herb mixture onto the top of each fillet.
4. **Bake:** Bake for 15-20 minutes or until the fish is cooked through and the crust is golden brown.
5. **Serve:** Serve with lemon wedges.

Teriyaki Salmon Skewers

Ingredients:

- 1 pound salmon fillet, cut into cubes
- 1/4 cup soy sauce
- 2 tablespoons honey
- 1 tablespoon rice vinegar
- 2 teaspoons sesame oil
- 1 teaspoon garlic, minced
- 1 teaspoon ginger, minced
- Skewers (soaked in water if wooden)

Instructions:

1. **Make Marinade:** In a bowl, whisk together soy sauce, honey, rice vinegar, sesame oil, garlic, and ginger.
2. **Marinate Salmon:** Add salmon cubes to the marinade and let sit for 30 minutes.
3. **Preheat Grill:** Preheat the grill to medium-high heat.
4. **Assemble Skewers:** Thread salmon cubes onto skewers.
5. **Grill:** Grill for 3-4 minutes on each side, basting with the marinade, until cooked through.
6. **Serve:** Serve with steamed rice and vegetables.

Clam Chowder

Ingredients:

- 4 slices bacon, diced
- 1 onion, diced
- 2 cloves garlic, minced
- 2 cups potatoes, diced
- 2 cups clam juice
- 1 cup heavy cream
- 2 cans (6.5 oz each) clams, drained and chopped
- Salt and pepper to taste
- Chopped parsley for garnish

Instructions:

1. **Cook Bacon:** In a large pot, cook bacon over medium heat until crispy. Remove and set aside, leaving the drippings in the pot.
2. **Sauté Vegetables:** Add onion and garlic to the pot, sautéing until softened.
3. **Add Potatoes and Broth:** Stir in potatoes and clam juice. Bring to a boil, then reduce heat and simmer until potatoes are tender (about 15 minutes).
4. **Add Cream and Clams:** Stir in heavy cream and chopped clams. Cook for an additional 5 minutes. Season with salt and pepper.
5. **Serve:** Top with crispy bacon and garnish with parsley.

Crab Cakes with Remoulade

Ingredients:

- 1 pound lump crab meat
- 1/2 cup breadcrumbs
- 1/4 cup mayonnaise
- 1 tablespoon Dijon mustard
- 1 egg, beaten
- 1 tablespoon Worcestershire sauce
- Salt and pepper to taste
- Oil for frying

Remoulade:

- 1/2 cup mayonnaise
- 1 tablespoon Dijon mustard
- 1 tablespoon lemon juice
- 1 tablespoon capers, chopped
- Salt and pepper to taste

Instructions:

1. **Make Remoulade:** In a small bowl, mix together mayonnaise, Dijon mustard, lemon juice, capers, salt, and pepper. Set aside.
2. **Make Crab Cakes:** In a large bowl, combine crab meat, breadcrumbs, mayonnaise, Dijon mustard, egg, Worcestershire sauce, salt, and pepper. Form into patties.
3. **Heat Oil:** In a skillet, heat oil over medium heat.
4. **Fry Crab Cakes:** Cook crab cakes for about 4-5 minutes on each side until golden brown.
5. **Serve:** Serve crab cakes with remoulade sauce on the side.

Pesto Baked Mahi-Mahi

Ingredients:

- 4 mahi-mahi fillets
- 1/2 cup basil pesto
- 1 tablespoon olive oil
- Salt and pepper to taste
- Grated Parmesan cheese for garnish

Instructions:

1. **Preheat Oven:** Preheat the oven to 375°F (190°C).
2. **Prepare Baking Dish:** Place mahi-mahi fillets in a greased baking dish.
3. **Add Pesto:** Spread pesto over the top of each fillet. Drizzle with olive oil and season with salt and pepper.
4. **Bake:** Bake for 15-20 minutes or until the fish is cooked through and flakes easily.
5. **Serve:** Garnish with grated Parmesan cheese and serve.

Fish Tacos with Chipotle Sauce

Ingredients:

- 1 pound white fish fillets (such as cod or tilapia)
- 1 teaspoon chili powder
- 1 teaspoon cumin
- Salt and pepper to taste
- 8 small corn tortillas
- 1 cup shredded cabbage
- 1/4 cup chopped cilantro

Chipotle Sauce:

- 1/2 cup mayonnaise
- 1-2 tablespoons adobo sauce (from canned chipotles)
- Juice of 1 lime

Instructions:

1. **Make Chipotle Sauce:** In a small bowl, combine mayonnaise, adobo sauce, and lime juice. Mix well and set aside.
2. **Season Fish:** Season fish fillets with chili powder, cumin, salt, and pepper.
3. **Cook Fish:** In a skillet, cook fish over medium heat for about 4-5 minutes on each side until cooked through.
4. **Warm Tortillas:** Warm tortillas in a dry skillet.
5. **Assemble Tacos:** Fill each tortilla with fish, shredded cabbage, and cilantro. Drizzle with chipotle sauce.
6. **Serve:** Serve immediately with lime wedges.

Enjoy preparing these delicious seafood dishes!

Grilled Sardines with Lemon and Parsley

Ingredients:

- 8 sardines, cleaned and gutted
- 2 tablespoons olive oil
- Juice of 1 lemon
- 2 tablespoons fresh parsley, chopped
- Salt and pepper to taste
- Lemon wedges for serving

Instructions:

1. **Preheat Grill:** Preheat your grill to medium-high heat.
2. **Prepare Sardines:** Rinse sardines under cold water and pat dry. In a bowl, combine olive oil, lemon juice, parsley, salt, and pepper.
3. **Coat Sardines:** Brush the sardines with the olive oil mixture, ensuring they are well coated.
4. **Grill:** Place sardines on the grill and cook for 3-4 minutes on each side, until cooked through and slightly charred.
5. **Serve:** Serve with lemon wedges and additional parsley for garnish.

Smoked Salmon Pasta

Ingredients:

- 8 ounces pasta (such as fettuccine or spaghetti)
- 1 tablespoon olive oil
- 1 shallot, minced
- 2 cloves garlic, minced
- 1 cup heavy cream
- 6 ounces smoked salmon, torn into pieces
- 1 tablespoon capers
- 1 tablespoon fresh dill, chopped
- Salt and pepper to taste
- Grated Parmesan cheese for serving

Instructions:

1. **Cook Pasta:** In a large pot of salted boiling water, cook pasta according to package instructions. Drain and set aside.
2. **Sauté Aromatics:** In a large skillet, heat olive oil over medium heat. Add shallot and garlic, sautéing until softened.
3. **Add Cream:** Stir in heavy cream, bringing to a simmer. Cook for 2-3 minutes until slightly thickened.
4. **Combine Ingredients:** Add smoked salmon, capers, dill, salt, and pepper. Stir in cooked pasta, tossing to combine.
5. **Serve:** Serve with grated Parmesan cheese on top.

Shrimp Scampi

Ingredients:

- 1 pound large shrimp, peeled and deveined
- 8 ounces linguine or spaghetti
- 4 tablespoons butter
- 4 cloves garlic, minced
- 1/2 teaspoon red pepper flakes (optional)
- Juice of 1 lemon
- 1/4 cup fresh parsley, chopped
- Salt and pepper to taste

Instructions:

1. **Cook Pasta:** In a pot of salted boiling water, cook linguine according to package instructions. Reserve 1/2 cup of pasta water, then drain the pasta.
2. **Sauté Shrimp:** In a large skillet, melt butter over medium heat. Add garlic and red pepper flakes, cooking until fragrant. Add shrimp and season with salt and pepper. Cook until shrimp are pink, about 3-4 minutes.
3. **Combine Ingredients:** Add cooked pasta to the skillet along with lemon juice and reserved pasta water. Toss to combine.
4. **Serve:** Garnish with fresh parsley and serve immediately.

Stuffed Flounder with Spinach and Feta

Ingredients:

- 4 flounder fillets
- 1 cup fresh spinach, chopped
- 1/2 cup feta cheese, crumbled
- 1/4 cup cream cheese, softened
- 1 clove garlic, minced
- 1 tablespoon lemon juice
- Salt and pepper to taste
- Olive oil for drizzling

Instructions:

1. **Preheat Oven:** Preheat the oven to 375°F (190°C).
2. **Prepare Filling:** In a bowl, combine spinach, feta cheese, cream cheese, garlic, lemon juice, salt, and pepper.
3. **Stuff Flounder:** Lay flounder fillets on a baking sheet. Place a spoonful of the spinach mixture on one end of each fillet and roll them up.
4. **Drizzle and Bake:** Drizzle with olive oil and bake for 15-20 minutes until the fish is cooked through.
5. **Serve:** Serve warm with a side salad.

Lemon Garlic Butter Scallops

Ingredients:

- 1 pound sea scallops
- 4 tablespoons butter
- 2 cloves garlic, minced
- Juice of 1 lemon
- Salt and pepper to taste
- Fresh parsley for garnish

Instructions:

1. **Prepare Scallops:** Pat scallops dry and season with salt and pepper.
2. **Heat Butter:** In a skillet over medium-high heat, melt butter. Add garlic and cook until fragrant.
3. **Sear Scallops:** Add scallops to the skillet, searing for 2-3 minutes on each side until golden brown and cooked through.
4. **Add Lemon Juice:** Squeeze lemon juice over scallops and toss to coat.
5. **Serve:** Garnish with fresh parsley and serve immediately.

Szechuan Spicy Shrimp

Ingredients:

- 1 pound shrimp, peeled and deveined
- 2 tablespoons vegetable oil
- 2 cloves garlic, minced
- 1 tablespoon ginger, minced
- 2 tablespoons Szechuan peppercorns
- 2 tablespoons soy sauce
- 2 tablespoons chili paste
- 1 tablespoon honey
- Chopped green onions for garnish

Instructions:

1. **Heat Oil:** In a large skillet or wok, heat vegetable oil over medium-high heat.
2. **Add Aromatics:** Add garlic, ginger, and Szechuan peppercorns, cooking until fragrant.
3. **Cook Shrimp:** Add shrimp and cook for about 3-4 minutes until they turn pink.
4. **Add Sauce:** Stir in soy sauce, chili paste, and honey, cooking for an additional 2 minutes.
5. **Serve:** Garnish with chopped green onions and serve with rice.

Baked Barramundi with Herb Butter

Ingredients:

- 4 barramundi fillets
- 4 tablespoons butter, softened
- 2 tablespoons fresh herbs (parsley, dill, or thyme), chopped
- Juice of 1 lemon
- Salt and pepper to taste

Instructions:

1. **Preheat Oven:** Preheat the oven to 375°F (190°C).
2. **Make Herb Butter:** In a bowl, combine softened butter, herbs, lemon juice, salt, and pepper.
3. **Prepare Fish:** Place barramundi fillets on a baking sheet. Spread herb butter over each fillet.
4. **Bake:** Bake for 15-20 minutes or until the fish is opaque and flakes easily.
5. **Serve:** Serve with lemon wedges and a side of vegetables.

Coconut Shrimp with Sweet Chili Sauce

Ingredients:

- 1 pound shrimp, peeled and deveined
- 1 cup shredded coconut
- 1 cup panko breadcrumbs
- 1/2 cup flour
- 2 eggs, beaten
- Oil for frying
- Sweet chili sauce for serving

Instructions:

1. **Prepare Breading Stations:** Set up three bowls: one with flour, one with beaten eggs, and one with a mixture of shredded coconut and panko breadcrumbs.
2. **Bread Shrimp:** Dredge each shrimp in flour, dip into the beaten eggs, and then coat with the coconut-panko mixture.
3. **Heat Oil:** In a large skillet, heat oil over medium-high heat.
4. **Fry Shrimp:** Fry shrimp for 2-3 minutes on each side until golden brown and cooked through.
5. **Serve:** Serve with sweet chili sauce for dipping.

Enjoy preparing these delicious seafood dishes!

Mediterranean Grilled Octopus

Ingredients:

- 2 pounds octopus, cleaned
- 1/4 cup olive oil
- Juice of 1 lemon
- 4 cloves garlic, minced
- 1 teaspoon smoked paprika
- Salt and pepper to taste
- Fresh parsley for garnish
- Lemon wedges for serving

Instructions:

1. **Boil Octopus:** In a large pot of salted water, boil octopus for about 45-60 minutes, or until tender. Drain and let cool.
2. **Prepare Marinade:** In a bowl, combine olive oil, lemon juice, garlic, paprika, salt, and pepper.
3. **Marinate:** Cut the octopus tentacles and place them in the marinade. Let marinate for at least 30 minutes.
4. **Preheat Grill:** Preheat the grill to medium-high heat.
5. **Grill Octopus:** Grill the marinated octopus for about 3-4 minutes on each side until charred.
6. **Serve:** Garnish with fresh parsley and serve with lemon wedges.

Sesame Crusted Ahi Tuna

Ingredients:

- 2 ahi tuna steaks (about 6 ounces each)
- 1/4 cup sesame seeds
- 2 tablespoons soy sauce
- 1 tablespoon olive oil
- 1 teaspoon wasabi paste (optional)
- Salt and pepper to taste
- Chopped green onions for garnish

Instructions:

1. **Season Tuna:** Season the tuna steaks with salt and pepper.
2. **Coat with Sesame Seeds:** Press both sides of each steak into the sesame seeds to coat.
3. **Heat Oil:** In a skillet, heat olive oil over medium-high heat.
4. **Sear Tuna:** Sear the tuna steaks for 1-2 minutes on each side for medium-rare, adjusting the time for your preferred doneness.
5. **Serve:** Slice the tuna and serve with soy sauce and wasabi, garnished with chopped green onions.

Fish Curry with Coconut Milk

Ingredients:

- 1 pound white fish (such as cod or tilapia), cut into pieces
- 1 can (14 oz) coconut milk
- 1 onion, chopped
- 2 cloves garlic, minced
- 1 tablespoon ginger, grated
- 2 tablespoons curry powder
- 1 tablespoon fish sauce
- 1 tablespoon lime juice
- Fresh cilantro for garnish
- Salt and pepper to taste

Instructions:

1. **Sauté Aromatics:** In a large pot, sauté onion, garlic, and ginger until softened.
2. **Add Spices:** Stir in curry powder and cook for another minute until fragrant.
3. **Add Coconut Milk:** Pour in coconut milk and bring to a simmer. Stir in fish sauce and lime juice.
4. **Cook Fish:** Add fish pieces and cook for 5-7 minutes, until the fish is cooked through.
5. **Serve:** Season with salt and pepper, and garnish with fresh cilantro.

Lobster Roll

Ingredients:

- 1 pound cooked lobster meat, chopped
- 1/4 cup mayonnaise
- 1 tablespoon lemon juice
- 1 tablespoon fresh chives, chopped
- Salt and pepper to taste
- 4 hot dog buns
- 2 tablespoons butter, melted

Instructions:

1. **Prepare Filling:** In a bowl, combine lobster meat, mayonnaise, lemon juice, chives, salt, and pepper.
2. **Toast Buns:** Brush hot dog buns with melted butter and toast them in a skillet until golden brown.
3. **Assemble Rolls:** Fill each toasted bun with the lobster mixture.
4. **Serve:** Serve immediately, garnished with extra chives if desired.

Crab Linguine with Garlic and Parsley

Ingredients:

- 8 ounces linguine
- 1 pound lump crab meat
- 4 tablespoons olive oil
- 4 cloves garlic, minced
- 1/4 cup fresh parsley, chopped
- Juice of 1 lemon
- Salt and pepper to taste
- Red pepper flakes (optional)

Instructions:

1. **Cook Pasta:** In a pot of salted boiling water, cook linguine according to package instructions. Reserve 1/2 cup of pasta water, then drain.
2. **Sauté Garlic:** In a large skillet, heat olive oil over medium heat. Add garlic and sauté until fragrant.
3. **Add Crab:** Gently fold in the crab meat, cooking just until warmed through.
4. **Combine Ingredients:** Add cooked linguine to the skillet along with lemon juice, parsley, reserved pasta water, salt, and pepper. Toss to combine.
5. **Serve:** Serve with additional parsley and red pepper flakes if desired.

Fish Tikka Masala

Ingredients:

- 1 pound white fish (like cod or tilapia), cut into cubes
- 1 cup yogurt
- 2 tablespoons tikka masala paste
- 1 tablespoon lemon juice
- 1 tablespoon vegetable oil
- 1 can (14 oz) coconut milk
- Fresh cilantro for garnish
- Salt and pepper to taste

Instructions:

1. **Marinate Fish:** In a bowl, combine yogurt, tikka masala paste, lemon juice, salt, and pepper. Add fish cubes and marinate for at least 30 minutes.
2. **Cook Fish:** In a skillet, heat vegetable oil over medium heat. Cook the marinated fish for 3-4 minutes until cooked through. Remove and set aside.
3. **Make Sauce:** In the same skillet, add coconut milk and bring to a simmer. Stir in additional tikka masala paste if desired.
4. **Combine:** Return the fish to the skillet and gently combine, cooking for an additional 2 minutes.
5. **Serve:** Garnish with fresh cilantro and serve with rice or naan.

Grilled Prawns with Garlic and Herbs

Ingredients:

- 1 pound large prawns, peeled and deveined
- 4 tablespoons olive oil
- 4 cloves garlic, minced
- 1 tablespoon fresh parsley, chopped
- 1 tablespoon fresh basil, chopped
- Juice of 1 lemon
- Salt and pepper to taste

Instructions:

1. **Prepare Marinade:** In a bowl, whisk together olive oil, garlic, parsley, basil, lemon juice, salt, and pepper.
2. **Marinate Prawns:** Add prawns to the marinade and let sit for 30 minutes.
3. **Preheat Grill:** Preheat the grill to medium-high heat.
4. **Grill Prawns:** Grill prawns for about 2-3 minutes on each side, until they turn pink and are cooked through.
5. **Serve:** Serve warm with extra lemon wedges.

Garlic Lemon Butter Mussels

Ingredients:

- 2 pounds mussels, cleaned and debearded
- 4 tablespoons butter
- 4 cloves garlic, minced
- 1/2 cup white wine
- Juice of 1 lemon
- Fresh parsley for garnish
- Salt and pepper to taste

Instructions:

1. **Sauté Garlic:** In a large pot, melt butter over medium heat. Add garlic and sauté until fragrant.
2. **Add Mussels:** Pour in white wine and bring to a simmer. Add mussels, cover the pot, and steam for 5-7 minutes until mussels open.
3. **Add Lemon Juice:** Remove from heat and squeeze lemon juice over the mussels. Season with salt and pepper.
4. **Serve:** Garnish with fresh parsley and serve with crusty bread for dipping.

Enjoy these flavorful seafood recipes!

Baked Salmon with Dill Cream Sauce

Ingredients:

- 4 salmon fillets
- Salt and pepper to taste
- 1 tablespoon olive oil
- 1 cup heavy cream
- 2 tablespoons fresh dill, chopped
- 1 tablespoon Dijon mustard
- Juice of 1 lemon
- Lemon wedges for serving

Instructions:

1. **Preheat Oven:** Preheat the oven to 375°F (190°C).
2. **Prepare Salmon:** Season salmon fillets with salt and pepper. Place them on a baking sheet lined with parchment paper. Drizzle with olive oil.
3. **Bake Salmon:** Bake for 15-20 minutes or until salmon is cooked through and flakes easily with a fork.
4. **Make Sauce:** While the salmon is baking, heat the heavy cream in a saucepan over medium heat. Stir in dill, Dijon mustard, and lemon juice. Simmer for 5 minutes until slightly thickened.
5. **Serve:** Drizzle the dill cream sauce over the baked salmon and serve with lemon wedges.

Fish en Papillote (Fish in Parchment)

Ingredients:

- 4 fish fillets (such as cod or halibut)
- 1 zucchini, thinly sliced
- 1 bell pepper, sliced
- 1 lemon, sliced
- 4 tablespoons olive oil
- Salt and pepper to taste
- Fresh herbs (like thyme or parsley), for garnish

Instructions:

1. **Preheat Oven:** Preheat the oven to 400°F (200°C).
2. **Prepare Parchment:** Cut four large pieces of parchment paper. Place each fish fillet in the center of a piece.
3. **Layer Vegetables:** Top each fillet with zucchini, bell pepper, and lemon slices. Drizzle with olive oil and season with salt and pepper.
4. **Seal Pouches:** Fold the parchment over the fish and crimp the edges to seal tightly.
5. **Bake:** Place the pouches on a baking sheet and bake for 15-20 minutes, until the fish is cooked through.
6. **Serve:** Carefully open the pouches and garnish with fresh herbs before serving.

Shrimp Fried Rice

Ingredients:

- 1 pound shrimp, peeled and deveined
- 3 cups cooked rice (preferably day-old)
- 2 eggs, beaten
- 1 cup mixed vegetables (peas, carrots, corn)
- 3 tablespoons soy sauce
- 2 tablespoons sesame oil
- 2 green onions, chopped
- Salt and pepper to taste

Instructions:

1. **Cook Eggs:** In a large skillet or wok, heat sesame oil over medium heat. Add the beaten eggs and scramble until cooked. Remove and set aside.
2. **Sauté Shrimp:** In the same skillet, add shrimp and cook until pink and opaque, about 3-4 minutes. Remove and set aside.
3. **Fry Rice:** Add the cooked rice to the skillet, breaking up any clumps. Stir-fry for 2-3 minutes until heated through.
4. **Add Veggies and Shrimp:** Add mixed vegetables, cooked shrimp, soy sauce, and scrambled eggs. Stir to combine and heat for another 2 minutes.
5. **Serve:** Garnish with chopped green onions and season with salt and pepper to taste.

Fish Stew with Fresh Herbs

Ingredients:

- 1 pound white fish (such as cod or snapper), cut into chunks
- 1 onion, chopped
- 2 cloves garlic, minced
- 1 can (14 oz) diced tomatoes
- 2 cups fish or vegetable broth
- 1 cup chopped fresh herbs (such as parsley, dill, or basil)
- 1 teaspoon paprika
- Salt and pepper to taste

Instructions:

1. **Sauté Onions:** In a large pot, sauté onions and garlic over medium heat until soft.
2. **Add Tomatoes and Broth:** Stir in diced tomatoes, broth, and paprika. Bring to a simmer.
3. **Add Fish:** Add fish chunks and cook for about 10 minutes until the fish is cooked through.
4. **Add Herbs:** Stir in fresh herbs and season with salt and pepper.
5. **Serve:** Serve hot with crusty bread.

Lemon Herb Grilled Swordfish

Ingredients:

- 4 swordfish steaks
- 1/4 cup olive oil
- Juice of 2 lemons
- 2 tablespoons fresh parsley, chopped
- 2 cloves garlic, minced
- Salt and pepper to taste

Instructions:

1. **Marinate Swordfish:** In a bowl, whisk together olive oil, lemon juice, parsley, garlic, salt, and pepper. Add swordfish steaks and marinate for 30 minutes.
2. **Preheat Grill:** Preheat the grill to medium-high heat.
3. **Grill Swordfish:** Remove swordfish from the marinade and grill for about 5-6 minutes on each side until cooked through.
4. **Serve:** Serve with extra lemon wedges and garnish with parsley if desired.

Crispy Fish Sandwiches

Ingredients:

- 4 white fish fillets (like tilapia or cod)
- 1 cup flour
- 1 cup cornmeal
- 2 eggs, beaten
- 1 cup buttermilk
- Salt and pepper to taste
- 4 sandwich buns
- Lettuce, tomato, and tartar sauce for serving

Instructions:

1. **Prepare Breading:** Set up a breading station with three bowls: flour seasoned with salt and pepper, beaten eggs, and cornmeal.
2. **Bread Fish:** Dip each fish fillet in flour, then in the beaten eggs, and finally coat with cornmeal.
3. **Fry Fish:** In a large skillet, heat oil over medium-high heat. Fry the breaded fish for 4-5 minutes on each side until golden brown and crispy.
4. **Assemble Sandwiches:** Place crispy fish on sandwich buns and top with lettuce, tomato, and tartar sauce.
5. **Serve:** Serve immediately.

Oysters Rockefeller

Ingredients:

- 12 fresh oysters, shucked
- 4 tablespoons butter
- 1 cup spinach, chopped
- 1/4 cup breadcrumbs
- 1/4 cup Parmesan cheese, grated
- 2 tablespoons fresh parsley, chopped
- 1 tablespoon lemon juice
- Salt and pepper to taste

Instructions:

1. **Preheat Oven:** Preheat the oven to 400°F (200°C).
2. **Sauté Spinach:** In a skillet, melt butter over medium heat. Add spinach and sauté until wilted. Remove from heat.
3. **Mix Topping:** In a bowl, combine sautéed spinach, breadcrumbs, Parmesan cheese, parsley, lemon juice, salt, and pepper.
4. **Top Oysters:** Place oysters on a baking sheet and spoon the mixture over each oyster.
5. **Bake:** Bake for 10-12 minutes until the topping is golden brown.
6. **Serve:** Serve hot.

Cajun Shrimp and Grits

Ingredients:

- 1 pound shrimp, peeled and deveined
- 1 cup grits
- 4 cups water or chicken broth
- 4 tablespoons butter
- 1 tablespoon Cajun seasoning
- 1/2 cup cheddar cheese, grated
- 1/4 cup green onions, chopped
- Salt and pepper to taste

Instructions:

1. **Cook Grits:** In a pot, bring water or broth to a boil. Stir in grits and reduce heat. Cook according to package instructions, stirring occasionally.
2. **Sauté Shrimp:** In a skillet, melt 2 tablespoons of butter over medium heat. Add shrimp and Cajun seasoning, cooking until shrimp is pink and cooked through, about 3-4 minutes.
3. **Add Cheese:** Once grits are cooked, stir in remaining butter and cheese until melted and creamy. Season with salt and pepper.
4. **Serve:** Spoon grits onto plates and top with sautéed shrimp. Garnish with chopped green onions.

Enjoy these delicious seafood recipes!

Grilled Fish Kebabs

Ingredients:

- 1 pound firm white fish (such as swordfish or halibut), cut into 1-inch cubes
- 1 bell pepper, cut into 1-inch pieces
- 1 red onion, cut into wedges
- 2 tablespoons olive oil
- Juice of 1 lemon
- 2 cloves garlic, minced
- Salt and pepper to taste
- Skewers (if using wooden skewers, soak in water for 30 minutes)

Instructions:

1. **Marinate Fish:** In a bowl, combine olive oil, lemon juice, garlic, salt, and pepper. Add fish cubes and toss to coat. Marinate for 15-30 minutes.
2. **Assemble Kebabs:** Thread fish, bell pepper, and onion onto skewers.
3. **Preheat Grill:** Preheat the grill to medium-high heat.
4. **Grill Kebabs:** Place the skewers on the grill and cook for 8-10 minutes, turning occasionally, until the fish is opaque and cooked through.
5. **Serve:** Serve hot with lemon wedges.

Thai Grilled Squid

Ingredients:

- 1 pound squid, cleaned and cut into rings
- 2 tablespoons soy sauce
- 1 tablespoon fish sauce
- 1 tablespoon lime juice
- 2 cloves garlic, minced
- 1 teaspoon sugar
- Fresh cilantro for garnish

Instructions:

1. **Marinate Squid:** In a bowl, whisk together soy sauce, fish sauce, lime juice, garlic, and sugar. Add squid rings and marinate for 15-30 minutes.
2. **Preheat Grill:** Preheat the grill to high heat.
3. **Grill Squid:** Thread squid onto skewers and grill for 2-3 minutes on each side until cooked through and slightly charred.
4. **Serve:** Garnish with fresh cilantro and serve with lime wedges.

Pan-Seared Sea Bass

Ingredients:

- 4 sea bass fillets
- Salt and pepper to taste
- 2 tablespoons olive oil
- 1 tablespoon butter
- Juice of 1 lemon
- Fresh herbs for garnish (such as parsley or dill)

Instructions:

1. **Season Fish:** Pat sea bass fillets dry and season with salt and pepper.
2. **Heat Pan:** In a skillet, heat olive oil over medium-high heat.
3. **Cook Fish:** Add fillets to the pan, skin-side down. Cook for 4-5 minutes until the skin is crispy. Flip and add butter to the pan, cooking for an additional 3-4 minutes.
4. **Serve:** Drizzle with lemon juice and garnish with fresh herbs before serving.

Clams Casino

Ingredients:

- 12 fresh clams, shucked and shells reserved
- 4 strips bacon, cooked and crumbled
- 1/4 cup breadcrumbs
- 1/4 cup bell pepper, finely chopped
- 2 tablespoons parsley, chopped
- 1 tablespoon lemon juice
- Salt and pepper to taste
- 2 tablespoons butter, melted

Instructions:

1. **Preheat Oven:** Preheat the oven to 375°F (190°C).
2. **Prepare Filling:** In a bowl, mix bacon, breadcrumbs, bell pepper, parsley, lemon juice, salt, and pepper.
3. **Stuff Clams:** Place the clam meat back in the shells and top with the breadcrumb mixture. Drizzle with melted butter.
4. **Bake:** Arrange the stuffed clams on a baking sheet and bake for 15-20 minutes until golden brown.
5. **Serve:** Serve hot as an appetizer.

Lobster Bisque

Ingredients:

- 2 lobsters (1.5 pounds each), cooked and meat removed
- 1/4 cup butter
- 1 onion, chopped
- 2 cloves garlic, minced
- 1 carrot, chopped
- 1 stalk celery, chopped
- 1/4 cup tomato paste
- 4 cups seafood or chicken broth
- 1 cup heavy cream
- Salt and pepper to taste
- Fresh chives for garnish

Instructions:

1. **Sauté Vegetables:** In a large pot, melt butter over medium heat. Add onion, garlic, carrot, and celery. Sauté until softened.
2. **Add Lobster:** Stir in lobster meat and cook for 2-3 minutes. Add tomato paste and broth, bringing to a simmer.
3. **Blend Soup:** Using an immersion blender, puree the soup until smooth. Stir in heavy cream and season with salt and pepper.
4. **Serve:** Garnish with fresh chives and serve hot.

Sautéed Garlic Shrimp with Spinach

Ingredients:

- 1 pound shrimp, peeled and deveined
- 2 tablespoons olive oil
- 4 cloves garlic, minced
- 4 cups fresh spinach
- Salt and pepper to taste
- Juice of 1 lemon

Instructions:

1. **Heat Oil:** In a large skillet, heat olive oil over medium heat.
2. **Sauté Garlic:** Add minced garlic and sauté for about 1 minute until fragrant.
3. **Cook Shrimp:** Add shrimp and cook for 3-4 minutes until they turn pink.
4. **Add Spinach:** Stir in spinach and cook until wilted. Season with salt, pepper, and lemon juice.
5. **Serve:** Serve immediately as a main dish or over rice.

Miso Glazed Cod

Ingredients:

- 4 cod fillets
- 1/4 cup miso paste
- 2 tablespoons sugar
- 2 tablespoons soy sauce
- 1 tablespoon rice vinegar
- 1 tablespoon sesame oil
- Sliced green onions for garnish

Instructions:

1. **Make Marinade:** In a bowl, whisk together miso paste, sugar, soy sauce, rice vinegar, and sesame oil.
2. **Marinate Cod:** Place cod fillets in a shallow dish and coat with the marinade. Cover and refrigerate for at least 30 minutes.
3. **Preheat Oven:** Preheat the oven to 400°F (200°C).
4. **Bake Cod:** Place marinated cod on a lined baking sheet and bake for 12-15 minutes until the fish is flaky and cooked through.
5. **Serve:** Garnish with sliced green onions and serve hot.

Enjoy preparing these delicious seafood dishes!

www.ingramcontent.com/pod-product-compliance
Lightning Source LLC
LaVergne TN
LVHW061954070526
838199LV00060B/4115

9798330476152